EXPLAINED

HAUNTED HOUSES

BY ADAM STONE

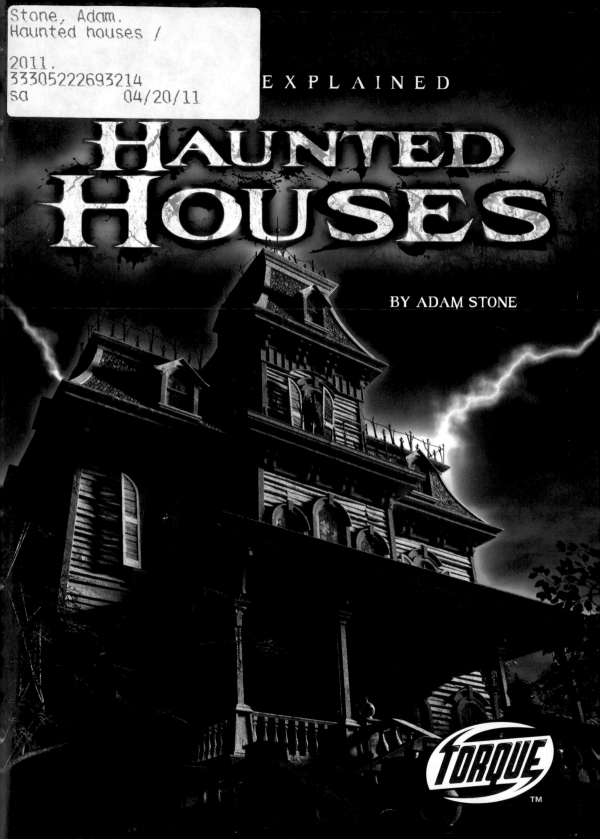

BELLWETHER MEDIA · MINNEAPOLIS, MN

Are you ready to take it to the extreme?
Torque books thrust you into the action-packed world
of sports, vehicles, mystery, and adventure. These books
may include dirt, smoke, fire, and dangerous stunts.
WARNING: read at your own risk.

Library of Congress Cataloging-in-Publication Data

Stone, Adam.
 Haunted houses / by Adam Stone.
   p. cm. -- (Torque : the unexplained)
 Includes bibliographical references and index.
 Summary: "Engaging images accompany information about haunted houses. The
combination of high-interest subject matter and light text is intended for students in grades 3
through 7"--Provided by publisher.
 ISBN 978-1-60014-501-8 (hardcover : alk. paper)
 1. Haunted houses--Juvenile literature. I. Title.
 BF1475.S76 2010
 133.1'22--dc22   2010011480

This edition first published in 2011 by Bellwether Media, Inc.

Printed in the United States of America, North Mankato, MN.

080110   1162

CONTENTS

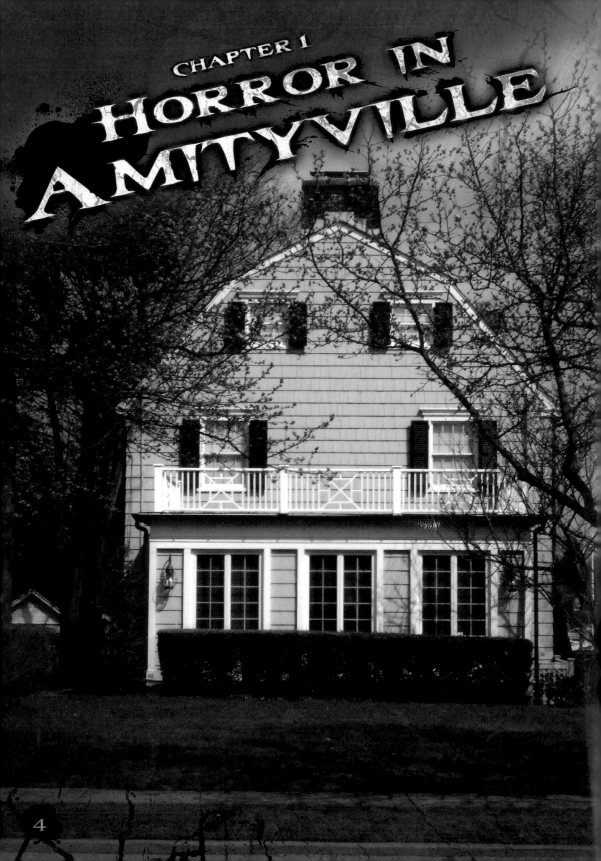

CHAPTER 1

HORROR IN AMITYVILLE

George and Kathy Lutz bought a home in Amityville, New York in 1975. The house looked very nice, but it had a dark history. Its previous owner had murdered his family and committed suicide.

George and Kathy Lutz

5

When the Lutz family moved in, strange things started to happen. Doors slammed without explanation and certain rooms were very cold. Terrible dreams of the suicide haunted Kathy as she slept. George claimed to see the shape of a **demon** in the fireplace. One of the children had an imaginary friend that looked like a demon.

The Lutz family became convinced that evil spirits were in their home. They tried to **bless** the house, but that did not help. The family feared for their safety. They left after only one month in the house and never returned. What was going on inside this house? Did evil spirits really **haunt** the home and want to drive the Lutz family away, or was it all their imaginations?

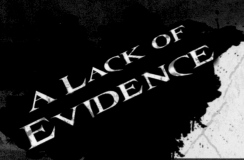

A LACK OF EVIDENCE

The story of the Lutz family became famous. People have studied the case and written books about it. No real proof of a haunting has ever been found. Many experts question the family's claims.

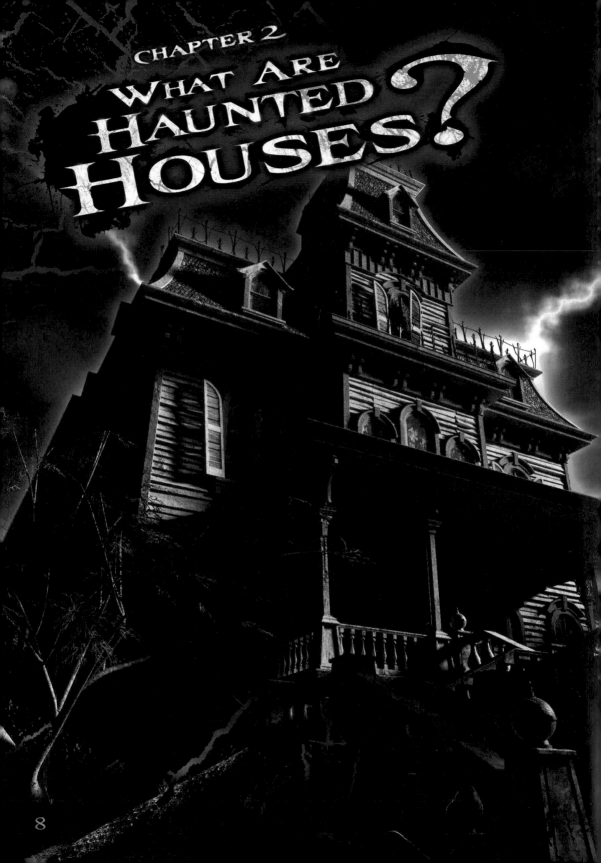

CHAPTER 2
WHAT ARE HAUNTED HOUSES?

Many people believe that spirits can haunt houses and other places. **Ghosts** might haunt some houses. Other houses may be haunted by evil spirits called demons.

Many people think a house can become haunted because of things that happened there in the past. They believe that if someone died in a house, that person's spirit could linger there. Believers think that many of these ghosts are harmless and often appear as faint shapes or lights.

Some reported ghosts are dangerous. **Poltergeists** are ghosts that people claim slam doors, move furniture, and break glass. Believers think the most dangerous type of haunting involves demons. They think these spirits haunt houses and try to hurt anyone who enters.

11

A spirit might haunt a house for a number of reasons. The spirit might not realize that it is dead. It may believe it still owns the house. A spirit may wish to communicate with the living or be angry and want revenge. There may be other reasons spirits haunt houses. No one knows exactly why a spirit might remain in a house.

Alcatraz

LOCK DOWN

Houses aren't the only buildings that can be haunted. Alcatraz was a famous prison in California. Many people claim to have heard ghostly sounds echoing through its empty halls.

FAMOUS HAUNTED HOUSES

House	Location
The Amityville Horror	New York
The White House	Washington, D.C.
Andleberry Estate	California
Lemp Mansion	Missouri
Old Louisville	Kentucky
Edinburgh Castle	Scotland
Temple Newsam	England
Arundel Castle	England

Description

Evil spirits are believed to haunt a house where
a man murdered his family and committed suicide.

The ghost of President Abraham Lincoln is believed
to haunt the White House.

This mansion was once a home for the insane;
it is believed to be home to many ghosts.

The ghosts of the Lemp family are said to haunt
this large mansion.

Many of the old homes in this neighborhood are said
to be haunted.

Many ghosts are believed to roam the tunnels
beneath this castle.

Many people claim to have seen the ghost of
"the Blue Lady" roaming the halls of this house.

At least four different ghosts have been seen in
this medieval castle.

ghost hunter

It is hard to prove that a house is truly haunted. **Ghost hunters** travel to places said to be haunted. They search for proof. Ghost hunters use **thermal cameras** to detect spirits, which are often very cold. They have special equipment to record very soft sounds. In a house, they listen for the whispers of spirits. Some even hold **séances**. They believe these ceremonies allow them to learn what spirits want and how to make a haunting stop.

17

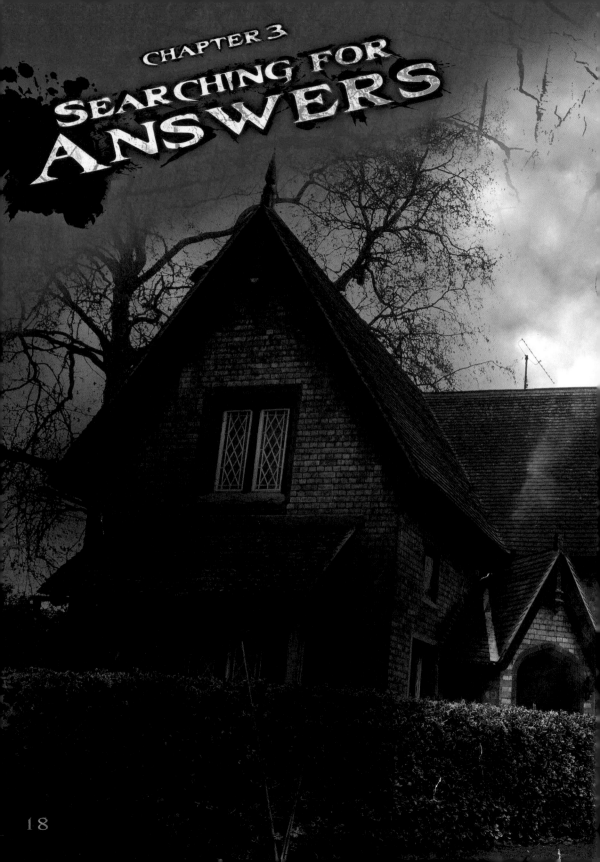

People can often find other explanations for haunted houses. **Carbon monoxide** can make people see and hear things that aren't really there. Mice can make strange sounds in walls. A house's **foundation** often settles and causes wood to creak and moan.

Do all strange noises and events in a house have simple explanations, or are there spirits involved? The next time your floorboards creak in the middle of the night, what will you think?

GET OUT OF MY HOUSE!

How do you get rid of a spirit? Some people try an exorcism. They believe that this religious ceremony will drive a spirit away from a place.

GLOSSARY

bless—to ask a higher power to cleanse or protect something

carbon monoxide—a poisonous gas that can cause people to hear or see things that are not present

demon—an ancient, powerful, and evil spirit

foundation—the lowest base of a building

ghost hunters—people who look for evidence of ghosts

ghosts—spirits; most ghosts are the spirits of people who have died.

haunt—for a ghost or spirit to linger in a specific place and make its presence known

poltergeists—ghosts that move objects

séances—ceremonies through which some people believe spirits of the dead can be contacted

thermal cameras—cameras that detect and show differences in temperature; ghost hunters use thermal cameras to detect ghosts.

TO LEARN MORE

AT THE LIBRARY

Brucken, Kelli M. *Haunted Houses*. San Diego, Calif.: KidHaven Press, 2006.

DeMolay, Jack. *Ghosts in Amityville: The Haunted House*. New York, N.Y.: PowerKids Press, 2007.

Stone, Adam. *Ghosts*. Minneapolis, Minn.: Bellwether Media, 2011.

ON THE WEB

Learning more about haunted houses is as easy as 1, 2, 3.

1. Go to www.factsurfer.com.

2. Enter "haunted houses" into the search box.

3. Click the "Surf" button and you will see a list of related Web sites.

With factsurfer.com, finding more information is just a click away.

INDEX

The images in this book are reproduced through the courtesy of: Jean-Marc Labal, front cover, pp. 8-9; Toby De Silva/Alamy, p. 4; Getty Images, p. 5; 3Dart, pp. 6-7; Juan Martinez, pp. 6-7, 20-21; Grischa Georgiew, pp. 10-11; Josu Sein Martinez, p. 12; Tom Hoenig/Visum/The Image Works, p. 13; Jill Battaglia, pp. 14-15; Andy Carpenean/AP Images, p. 16 (small); Dale A. Stork, pp. 16-17; Ted Kinsman/Photolibrary, p. 17; Sean Nei, pp. 18-19; Eric Isselee, p. 19 (small).